VIDEO GAME
ADDICTION

By P.J. Graham

ReferencePoint
Press®

San Diego, CA

For more information, contact:
ReferencePoint Press, Inc.
PO Box 27779
San Diego, CA 92198
www.ReferencePointPress.com

APR 0 9 2019

LIBRARY OF CONGRESS CATALOGING-IN-PUBLICATION DATA

Names: Graham, P.J., author.
Title: Video Game Addiction / by P.J. Graham.
Description: San Diego, CA : ReferencePoint Press, Inc., 2019. | Series:
   The world of video games | Audience: Grade 9 to 12. | Includes
   bibliographical references and index.
Identifiers: LCCN 2018038251 (print) | LCCN 2018038680 (ebook) | ISBN
   9781682825600 (ebook) | ISBN 9781682825594 (hardback)
Subjects: LCSH: Video game addiction--Juvenile literature. | Video
   games--Psychological aspects--Juvenile literature. | Video games--Social
   aspects--Juvenile literature.
Classification: LCC RC569.5.V53 (ebook) | LCC RC569.5.V53 G76 2019 (print) | DDC
   616.85/84--dc23
LC record available at https://lccn.loc.gov/2018038251

CONTENTS

IMPORTANT EVENTS IN THE HISTORY OF
VIDEO GAMES

1981
D.N. Rushton coins the phrase *"Space Invaders* epilepsy" to describe light-induced seizures from playing video games.

1994
The video game industry creates the Entertainment Software Rating Board (ESRB) in response to US Senate hearings on violence in video games.

1958
Physicist William Higinbotham creates the first video game, *Tennis for Two*.

| 1960 | 1970 | 1980 | 1990 | 2000 |

1975
Three years after the arcade version of *Pong* was released, Atari begins selling the home version.

1995
Sony sells the PlayStation console in the United States at a much lower price than the competition, making the system affordable to more players.

1982
Eighteen-year-old Peter Burkowski dies of a heart attack after playing the *Berzerk* arcade video game.

1989
The release of Nintendo's Game Boy makes high-quality games portable.

2013
The American Psychiatric Association (APA) adds Internet Gaming Addiction as a condition for further study.

2016
Pokémon Go becomes a summer hit and invites people to spend many hours hunting for virtual creatures on their cell phones.

2009
Casual gamers start playing games such as *Farmville* and *Angry Birds* on their cell phones and mobile devices.

2010
A South Korean couple is arrested for the death of their child, whom they neglected while playing video games.

| 2000 | 2005 | 2010 | 2015 | 2020 |

1999
EverQuest popularizes online multiplayer games.

2009
Four years after its release, *World of Warcraft* becomes the most popular massively multiplayer online (MMO) game with 11.5 million players.

2018
The World Health Organization (WHO) adds Gaming Disorder to the 2018 International Classification of Diseases

ADDICTION AND
RECOVERY

In October 2015, twenty-seven-year-old Charlie Bracke entered rehab. He wasn't an alcoholic or addicted to drugs. He didn't spend hours gambling in a casino. Bracke was addicted to video games.

Bracke escaped to video games when he was young to avoid being bullied by his older brother. He used the games to zone out and escape his problems. Over the next few years, his video game use rose and fell. But during his college years, Bracke's gaming became excessive. He would skip classes to play video games. After his grandmother died, he played even more. Sometimes he would play fifty to sixty hours of games per week.

Bracke stopped playing games with his family's help. However, after moving across the United States to take a new job, he began gaming again. Bracke would play video games instead of going to work. He said, "I would wake up in the morning and get on the computer, telling myself I'd just play one game and then go to work. Next thing I knew, it'd be 3:00 in the afternoon, and I still hadn't showered or gotten ready for the day."[1]

When Bracke believed he couldn't break the cycle of video game addiction, he felt hopeless. According to Bracke, "I felt like I was not a worthy human being. . . . Luckily, my parents came to visit and

Some people can play video games safely. Other people may develop an addiction to video games.

could tell something was seriously wrong. . . . We started researching treatment facilities right away."[2]

Bracke entered the ReSTART Life rehab facility near Seattle, Washington. There, he created a plan for handling technology and building healthy routines. After almost seven weeks, he left the facility with coping strategies to manage his video game addiction.

Bracke was a grown man with a home, a job, and a good work ethic. He had overcome video game overuse in his youth. But he still fell back into a harmful video game habit in order to escape his troubles. For young people struggling with school, peer pressure, and anxiety about their lives, resisting and dealing with this addiction can be difficult. After all, unlike many other addictions, video games are legal for all ages. They are readily available on almost any digital device.

VIDEO GAME ADDICTION

Video game addiction (VGA) goes by many names depending on who you ask. It has been called internet gaming disorder, gaming disorder, and pathological gaming, among other things. Whatever one decides to call it, VGA is changing the way we look at video games. Overuse of digital entertainment has the potential to derail bright futures.

Whether video game addiction truly is an addiction is a hot topic of debate. Some people point to the brain's reward center and release of the feel-good chemical dopamine as the root of the problem. Others insist that the real culprits are disorders that are both masked and escaped by playing video games.

Dr. Petros Levounis, chairman of the psychology department at Rutgers New Jersey Medical School, sees what he believes are addiction symptoms in some gamers. Levounis says, "I have patients who come in suffering from an addiction to *Candy Crush Saga*, and they're substantially similar to people who come in with a cocaine disorder. Their lives are ruined, their interpersonal relationships suffer, their physical condition suffers."[3]

However, Jackson Toby, a professor of sociology at Rutgers University, does not believe that the word *addiction* is correct. He states:

> "I have patients who come in suffering from an addiction to *Candy Crush Saga*, and they're substantially similar to people who come in with a cocaine disorder."[3]
>
> –Dr. Petros Levounis, psychologist

It only describes strong temptations; it does not explain strong temptations. What makes the temptation so strong? The memory of past pleasant experiences with the behavior that we are talking about, in this case video games. I don't believe that someone can be addicted to video games.[4]

There are differences in the treatment for video game addiction from other types of addiction. Some experts believe in a strict no-technology stance where technology is banned entirely. Others focus on empathy and teaching a healthy tech-life balance, as most people cannot avoid all technology in their lives.

VGA IN THE UNITED STATES

Until 2017, medical officials in the United States were resistant to labeling VGA as a disorder. This limited the funding available to research the issue. But in 2017, the National Institutes of Health (NIH) funded its first study on internet addiction, which included online gaming. According to Dr. Nancy Petry, the lead researcher of the study, "A lot of people have developed such severe problems with gaming. There is evidence that they are dropping out of school; they are losing their jobs; they are losing their families."[5]

While doctors and researchers debate video games, their use is already affecting society. Parents question the types of technology in their homes and schools. People worry about balancing their digital lives with real-world interactions. Those who play games a lot are changing their brains and bodies. Those with depression, anxiety, and other disorders may need special help to avoid game addiction. Meanwhile, educators have found that video games can also be a helpful learning tool. More studies are needed to make clear how video games can both positively and negatively affect people's lives.

WHAT IS VIDEO GAME
ADDICTION?

VGA has become an important issue in recent years. Gamers who are addicted may act out if their gaming time is challenged or limited, lie about how much they are playing, or have outbursts of anger if interrupted. They are obsessed with gaming and will have withdrawal symptoms when they aren't gaming. Essentially, they cannot function properly without video games.

It is a controversial topic. Psychologists, parents, and gaming enthusiasts have differing viewpoints on VGA. There are reports of people pushing their bodies to exhaustion and even death while playing video games. Some parents hide or lock up digital devices to prevent their children from playing all night. Adults have even lost their jobs when they cannot focus at work. Losing a job and income can lead to a person losing his or her home. Spending too much time gaming can interfere with a person's relationships with families and friends. Meanwhile, psychologists and researchers debate what to call the problem and how to treat it.

THE POPULARITY OF VIDEO GAMES

Video gaming is not a niche hobby. It has become a mainstream form of entertainment. A wide variety of games in assorted genres appeal

Someone may have a video game addiction if he or she cannot function without video games. The person may also have a hard time doing chores or other tasks instead of playing video games.

to all types of players. Some enjoy playing sophisticated games with high-tech graphics on gaming computers. Others sit in front of a TV and play console games online with friends. And some people might only play simple games on their smartphones while sitting in waiting rooms or standing in lines.

As of 2015, 49 percent of people in the United States play video games regularly. Broken down by gender, about 50 percent of men and 48 percent of women reported playing video games. Forty-eight percent of US homes have a game console, and 22 percent have a handheld gaming system. Many other homes, though they lack dedicated gaming devices, have computers, tablets, and smartphones that can also be used to play games.

HOURS SPENT PLAYING VIDEO GAMES

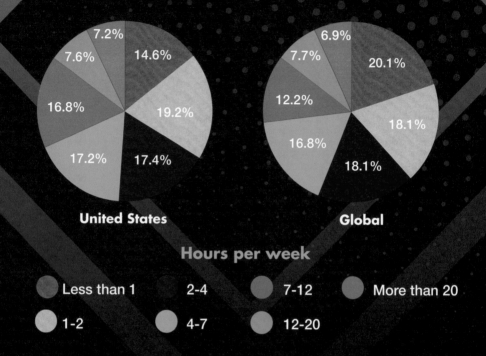

United States

Global

Hours per week

- Less than 1
- 1-2
- 2-4
- 4-7
- 7-12
- 12-20
- More than 20

A 2018 survey in the United States showed that people in the United States play an average of 6.44 hours of video games per week. The global average is 5.96 hours per week. Additionally, the survey noted that in the United States, gamers on average play for 1 hour and 22 minutes at a time, but "globally, gamers play consecutively for an average of [1] hour and 20 minutes at a time." Gaming is an engaging hobby because many video games are designed to tap into the reward system of the brain. It feels good to play, and this encourages gamers to play for longer periods.

"The State of Online Gaming—2018," LimeLight Networks, 2018. www.limelight.com.

WHEN DOES A HOBBY BECOME AN ADDICTION?

Experts continue to debate when gaming goes from being a hobby to being a problem or even an addiction. One area of focus has been online games, in which players cooperate or compete with other gamers over the internet. In 2013, the American Psychiatric Association (APA) added Internet Gaming Disorder (IGD) as a "condition for further study" to the fifth edition of the *Diagnostic and Statistical Manual of Mental Disorders*, or *DSM*.[6] The *DSM* is a reference text used by mental health providers to help ensure consistent diagnoses of mental disorders. The APA lists nine different criteria for IGD. It says that someone should display five or more of these criteria within a period of one year before being considered addicted to video games.

The first criterion is a preoccupation with video games or internet-based games. This means the person thinks about gaming so much that the thoughts control his life. The person cannot think of or plan for anything except playing games. The second sign is showing symptoms of withdrawal when the person doesn't have access to games. These symptoms can include being anxious, grumpy, or sad because she isn't able to play. For example, many young people with video game addiction will get depressed or even aggressive if parents take away their ability to game.

A third symptom is known as game tolerance. This means the person has built up his ability to play for long periods of time. He will play more and more video games to feel satisfied. Fourth, those suffering from the disorder may have unsuccessfully tried to control or reduce their time spent playing games. Fifth, people with addiction to video games may lose interest in real-world things such

Playing video games triggers the brain's reward system. This makes people feel happy.

as relationships, hobbies, sports, and other forms of entertainment. A sixth indication is that while a person may realize he has a problem, he continues to play games excessively. The seventh criterion is that he may also lie to others about time spent playing video games.

The eighth sign of IGD is using games to escape from life or to soothe emotions such as anxiety or guilt. It may be easier to control the video game than it is to control events in real life. This can make a video game comforting. Finally, the ninth criterion is that the person has risked losing relationships, jobs, or school opportunities because of how much time she spends playing video games. This is especially true of those who play massively multiplayer online games (MMOs), which often involve playing with other gamers in scheduled in-game events. These can take hours or days of a person's time per week. As this commitment grows, other relationships and activities are not given the time and attention needed.

Leading addiction expert Dr. Nicholas Kardaras believes that increases in video game use are dangerous. In a 2016 article in the *New York Post*, Kardaras equated video games to "digital heroin."[7] Dopamine, a chemical that helps to control the brain's reward and pleasure centers, is released in the brain while playing video games. It is also released when taking certain drugs, such as heroin.

Kardaras adds, "Your kid's brain on *Minecraft* looks like a brain on drugs. . . . In addition, hundreds of clinical studies show that screens increase depression, anxiety, and aggression and can even lead to psychotic-like features where the video gamer loses touch with reality."[8]

Symptoms of addiction may be clear to friends and family, but they may not be obvious to the gamer with an addiction. Gamers do not always see their playing accurately. For example, 49 percent of people in the United States play some form of video game, whether on a gaming console, arcade cabinet, computer, or cell phone. However, only 10 percent of people consider themselves to be gamers. This could make it hard for people to even realize that they might have a problem with video games.

> **"Your kid's brain on *Minecraft* looks like a brain on drugs."** [8]
>
> –Dr. Nicholas Kardaras, psychologist

HOW SERIOUS IS VGA?

VGA is not a clear-cut issue even among medical and psychiatric professionals. Dr. Peter Gray is a research professor at Boston College. He is an expert on the role of play in learning. Gray says that Kardaras's theory greatly exaggerates the effect of dopamine on a player's brain. Psychologist Chris Ferguson agrees. He states

There are many myths such as that games involve dopamine and brain regions similar to substance abuse. There's a kernel of truth to that but only insofar as any pleasurable activity activates these regions. How gaming involves them is more similar to other fun activities like eating chocolate . . . getting a good grade, etc., not heroin or cocaine.[9]

Some experts do not think VGA is a true addiction, while others claim it is a behavioral addiction like gambling or binge eating. Others prefer to say video games are simply overused. What remains clear is that the population of gamers is huge and continues to rise. According to a 2018 survey by the Entertainment Software Association, 60 percent of people in the United States play video games every day.

Researchers also do not agree on how many people struggle with compulsive video gaming. Some, like Ferguson, say that the *DSM* criteria used to define IGD are not useful. For example, one of the criteria involves using games to feel good and improve mood. But any other hobbies, such as sports, knitting, or building models, might be used for the same effect, and no one would classify an interest in those things as a disorder. Ferguson suggests that only 1 to 3 percent of gamers let their hobby interfere with life responsibilities. Other researchers suggest the figure is higher, ranging from 8 to 10 percent. Researchers in other countries have found a variety of higher or lower figures, including 2.4 percent in China and 19.1 percent in Hong Kong.

Mental health professionals can help people with addictions. But some professionals do not consider VGA to be a true addiction.

These differences seem to be based not only in the popularity of games in a particular place, but also in how gaming addiction is defined, diagnosed, and measured.

Dr. Gray also discusses weaknesses in five of the nine criteria that the APA lists for IGD. He notes that most people think a lot about things they are passionate about. Many people also use hobbies to reduce stress and anxiety. Gray also provides another reason for why gamers might feel compelled to lie about how long they play video games: many people tend to disapprove of playing games for extended periods. "What I'm suggesting here is that a person who has a quite healthy passion for video gaming, who is not at all

> **❝If someone is restless when not able to play, is losing significant relationships or meaningful employment because of gaming, feels that gaming is causing more harm than benefit, and yet is unable to stop—then that person has a problem.❞** [11]
>
> *–Dr. Peter Gray, psychologist*

suffering, could very well check off these five 'symptoms' and thereby get a diagnosis of IGD," Gray says.[10]

Still, Gray recognizes that it is very possible for people to have an unhealthy relationship with gaming. He says, "If someone is restless when not able to play, is losing significant relationships or meaningful employment because of gaming, feels that gaming is causing more harm than benefit, and yet is unable to stop—then that person has a problem."[11]

THE ADDICTION DEBATE

Writing about how people disagree about the value of children playing *Minecraft*, author Jolyon Jenkins implies with some humor that the debate will never end. Each side continues to find excuses that justify their beliefs. Jenkins says, "The opposition implies that it is just the latest moral panic, and that Stone Age elders probably thought the world was going to the dogs when people stopped just staring at the fires and started telling each other stories."[12] He is reluctant to use the word *addicted* for young children who play a lot of *Minecraft*, comparing the interactions in *Minecraft* to things someone might experience while reading a book. This suggests that just because the

DYING TO GAME

In 1982, an eighteen-year-old man named Peter Bukowski died while playing the popular arcade game *Berzerk*. Playing at an Indiana shopping mall, Bukowski earned a few high-ranking scores in *Berzerk* twice in fifteen minutes, then collapsed and died soon after of a heart attack. This is often described as one of the first video game–related deaths. However, medical experts believed that Bukowski had a pre-existing heart condition. It is unlikely the game played a role in killing him.

Since then, several other people have died while playing video games. In 2015, a man in Taiwan died of a heart attack after a three-day gaming binge. In 2016, twenty-year-old British gamer Chris Staniforth died of deep vein thrombosis, which is a blood clot that forms due to lack of movement. Staniforth was known to play up to 12 hours of video games at a time.

Journalist Simon Parkin, author of *Death by Video Game*, looks at factors in video game–related deaths. However, he noted that these stories are not unique to video games, and that they can happen with any "sedentary pursuit." "You can die from a Netflix binge, and I'm sure people have. But there is something unique about video games that I can see in my own life," Parkin said in an interview. "I'm much more likely to sit and play a game for a whole day than I am most other entertainment activities."

Quoted in Damon Beres, "Why People Die Playing Video Games," Huffington Post, August 14, 2015. www.huffingtonpost.com.

technology changes, the basic process of creating and experiencing stories is still the same.

One reason people disagree about video game addiction is that no substance is taken into the body to feed the addiction, as is seen with alcohol, cigarettes, and illegal drugs. These substances create a chemical addiction in the person taking them. They cause physical withdrawal symptoms, such as vomiting, headaches, and fevers, if the

Video games can be a fun activity to share with friends. Many people can play video games without it developing into an addiction.

user suddenly stops using them. These symptoms make it hard for people to stop taking drugs. Video game addiction does not involve such physical symptoms. Instead, it is a behavioral addiction. Another prevalent behavioral addiction is gambling. For many decades, mental health practitioners treated excessive gambling as an impulse control disorder rather than an addiction. However, author Ferris Jabr notes similarities to drug addiction in an article for *Scientific American*:

> *Research to date shows that pathological gamblers and drug addicts share many of the same genetic predispositions for impulsivity and reward seeking. Just as substance addicts require increasingly strong hits to get high, compulsive gamblers pursue ever riskier ventures. Likewise, both*

drug addicts and problem gamblers endure symptoms of withdrawal when separated from the chemical or thrill they desire.[13]

If VGA is also a behavioral addiction, then people who are addicted to video games may also have those genetic predispositions. Additionally, people with behavioral or substance addictions often also have other mental health issues such as depression or anxiety.

However, doctors Lawrence Kutner and Cheryl K. Olson explain that it is not clear that video game overuse fits the criteria of a true addiction: "Their game playing behavior may be out of their control and interfering with their lives, but the underlying mechanism may be different than that of someone addicted to a drug."[14] Many other doctors and psychologists echo this sentiment, pointing to the possibility of other underlying disorders that cause people to become too focused on games instead of real life.

For all types of addiction, experts usually point out another element: lack of connection to things in the real world. This includes relationships, a fulfilling job, and other interests. Such is the case of "Evan," an anonymous man interviewed for the book *Glued to Games*

> **"Their game playing behavior may be out of their control and interfering with their lives, but the underlying mechanism may be different than that of someone addicted to a drug."** [14]
>
> *–Dr. Lawrence Kutner and Dr. Cheryl K. Olson, authors of* Grand Theft Childhood

by Scott Rigby and Richard M. Ryan. At twenty-seven, Evan was a part-time student who lived with his dad. He was not motivated to keep a job or maintain personal hygiene. However, Evan devoted his life to video games. He had given up on a normal life. According to Rigby and Ryan:

> His overuse is related to the fact that he both loves games and also loves little else. There is a gap there in which the need satisfactions he achieves in games far outstrip his experience in other aspects of life. Like a black hole, he feels an irresistible pull into games, even though, in his own words, he feels that time spent there disappears into the blackness and "doesn't amount to anything."[15]

HELP FOR GAMING DISORDER

In 2018, the World Health Organization (WHO) included gaming disorder in its International Classification of Diseases. Many psychologists expressed concern that this decision was based on incorrect comparisons to drug addiction. Others worried that the classification may not get to the root of the problem with excessive video gaming. Psychologist Andrew Przybylski thinks that the WHO decision may "[stigmatize] millions of players and may divert limited mental health resources from core psychiatric problems such as depression or anxiety which might be at the heart of problematic play."[16]

Others see the disorder's inclusion as helpful for the people who overuse games to the point of physical harm, job loss, or lost relationships. According to Cosette Rae, cofounder of the ReSTART treatment facility for internet and gaming addiction, the designation could help people for several reasons. Rae says it can be difficult for people to get treatment for excessive gaming, and it is especially difficult to get that treatment covered by insurance. She says, "Because people don't understand [video game addiction], they haven't regarded it as a real problem. They dismiss what this person is experiencing."[17]

Regardless of precisely how video game addiction is defined and diagnosed, it is likely that as video game use increases overall, more people will overuse video games. As more researchers study this phenomenon and gain a better understanding of what video games do to our brains, they will find better ways to help people who feel their gaming habits are out of control.

> **"Because people don't understand [video game addiction], they haven't regarded it as a real problem. They dismiss what this person is experiencing."** [17]
>
> –Cosette Rae, cofounder of the ReSTART treatment facility

HOW DOES VIDEO GAME ADDICTION AFFECT THE **BRAIN AND BODY?**

Understanding the nature of video game addiction or overuse is not a simple matter. Playing video games affects a person's brain and body in both positive and negative ways. Researchers are searching for how people might gain the benefits of video games while avoiding the negative effects. As in many parts of life, striking the right balance is key to a healthy lifestyle.

THE REWARD CIRCUIT

The human brain is remarkably complex, and video games affect it in many ways. One of the most significant ways is that games can take advantage of the brain's reward circuit. The brain has billions of neurons, which are cells that are connected across the brain. The neurons send signals that tell the brain and body to do different things. They can send signals to nerves anywhere in the body. In order to send these signals, neurons use chemicals called neurotransmitters.

One type of neurotransmitter is dopamine. Dopamine is released during pleasurable activities such as playing video games. However, dopamine is also released when people use some illegal

Dopamine and the Reward Circuit

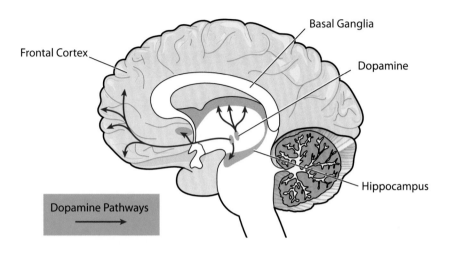

Dopamine travels through the brain's reward circuit and makes people feel good. This chemical is released when people play video games.

substances, such as cocaine. According to the National Institute on Drug Abuse (NIDA):

> *A burst of dopamine signals that something important is happening that needs to be remembered. This dopamine signal causes changes in neural connectivity that make it easier to repeat the activity again and again without thinking about it, leading to the formation of habits. . . . Drugs produce . . . larger surges of dopamine, powerfully reinforcing the connection between consumption of the drug, the resulting pleasure, and all the external cues linked to the experience.*[18]

This cycle of motivation and reward happens in the basal ganglia, which is also known as the reward circuit. Some drugs "over-activate this circuit, producing the euphoria of the drug high," according to NIDA.[19] This leads to the compulsive behavior and addiction.

TOO MUCH OF A GOOD THING

When people play action games, the brain releases large quantities of dopamine as well as another neurotransmitter, norepinephrine. Both of these chemicals are connected to learning and to addiction. Many people point directly to dopamine as the culprit for turning healthy people into compulsive gamers. They even state that gaming is as addictive as illegal substances because of dopamine. The idea of getting addicted to online games has been present in the gaming community for many years, with gamers jokingly referring to *EverQuest*, one of the earliest MMOs, as "EverCrack."

Over time, the brain adjusts to large quantities of dopamine and corrects itself. According to NIDA, the brain does this by "producing fewer neurotransmitters in the reward circuit, or by reducing the number of receptors that can receive signals. As a result, the person's ability to experience pleasure from naturally rewarding . . . activities is also reduced."[20] This may cause a person to feel depressed or unable to enjoy things they used to find pleasurable. They may need to use more drugs, or play more video games, to achieve the same effect. This creates a cycle of use and addiction as a person develops a tolerance.

According to Kardaras, "Recent brain imaging research is showing that [games] affect the brain's frontal cortex—which controls executive functioning, including impulse control—in exactly the same way that cocaine does."[21] Similar statements are echoed by others, though in less dramatic ways. Business and technology writer Jack Flanagan says, "Video games are built to exploit this part of our brain.

Kill monster, get points. Complete level, get happy music. Win game, feel satisfied. It's a very simple and primitive part of who we are."[22]

Others experts disagree that the release of dopamine proves that people are addicted to video games. Dr. Peter Gray notes that the studies Kardaras refers to show that video game playing releases dopamine and that heroin activates the same paths in the brain. However, Gray says, "If video gaming didn't increase activity in these dopaminergic pathways, we would have to conclude that video gaming is no fun."[23] Eating a slice of pizza releases roughly the same amount of dopamine as gaming. By comparison, a drug like meth can release ten times that amount. Gray suggests that focusing on dopamine misses the bigger problem with video game addiction.

> **"Kill monster, get points. Complete level, get happy music. Win game, feel satisfied. It's a very simple and primitive part of who we are." [22]**
>
> –Jack Flanagan, writer

NEED SATISFACTIONS

In *Glued to Games*, authors Scott Rigby and Richard Ryan point to three "need satisfactions" as a primary reason video games can become addictive. They explain that video games satisfy our needs with immediacy, consistency, and density.

Immediacy refers to how quickly someone can fulfill a need. Rigby and Ryan note that playing games with friends in their childhood took time and effort to organize. They write: "A ballgame required at least an hour of door-knocking to see who was home and willing to play. Even then you might not get a quorum."[24] Though people can organize activities with cell phones, tablets, and computers, it still takes time to

Sports video games can be played with many people. It may be easier for someone to find people to play with in the digital world than in the real world.

get everyone in the group to agree on what to do, when to do it, and where to do it. By comparison, video games meet this need almost immediately, according to the authors. They explain, "It is just easier to connect to a digital world than to many activities in the molecular world, creating a legitimate temptation to always turn there first."[25]

The second advantage of video games is consistency, or how regularly the activity meets someone's needs. Video games run by a set of rules that players follow in order to be rewarded. As long as the player follows these rules, he or she will satisfy a need. Rigby and Ryan admit that life doesn't always give us the rewards we want. They add, "But for those who are struggling with these challenges more chronically, the allure of predictable and consistent virtual worlds can be particularly strong."[26]

The final advantage is density, or how often the need is met. Video games give players consistent feedback on how well they are doing. Levels, maps, and achievements show how the players are progressing through the game. This progress is often shown in percentages, and players can receive extra achievements for completing 100 percent of a level or entire game. This feedback allows the player to meet and track their needs every step of the way, not just once the game is finished.

The desire to finish a game is something that game designers use to keep players coming back to the video game over and over. This is called the Zeigarnik effect. In 1927, Russian psychologist Bluma Zeigarnik observed that waiters in restaurants were able to remember orders until the order was completed. Then their memory let go of

OUR BRAINS NEED TO PLAY

Scientists have long known that play is important to a child's development. Siobhan O'Connor, author of the *Time* magazine article "The Secret Power of Play," stated that play helps more than just the body. She wrote, "Play teaches children how to work together and, at the same time, how to be alone. It teaches them how to be human."

Humans learn by playing. Neuroscientist Jaak Panksepp says that many animals are restless. They have a drive to explore the world and find the things they need to survive. Panksepp believes that play causes humans to be curious of their surroundings for both fun and intellectual pursuits. This curiosity helps humans adapt to new situations. O'Connor adds, "Children who can entertain themselves, or play with one another, are unconsciously learning how to adapt themselves to challenges they'll face further down the road."

Siobhan O'Connor, "The Secret Power of Play," Time, September 6, 2017.

the information. In short, they could remember something better while it was in process rather than after the process was complete.

Psychologists believe that humans experience tension and intrusive thoughts when something is left incomplete. They also believe that when we complete a goal, we experience relief and even pleasure. By always having one or more new quests for a gamer to achieve or secrets to unlock, game designers keep players from permanently putting down a video game. Rigby and Ryan explain, "MMOs are designed so that your list of tasks is never done. . . . As soon as you finish or 'turn in' a quest, you are immediately offered another one with an even bigger reward."[27]

> **"As soon as you finish or 'turn in' a quest, you are immediately offered another one with an even bigger reward."** [27]
>
> –Scott Rigby and Richard Ryan, authors of Glued to Games

READING COMPREHENSION

Students who play games or read about games for several hours a week may not be addicted to video games—they may be learning to read. While some experts say that video games are harmful to maturing brains, others suggest that video games can actually help struggling readers. According to an article by Clive Thompson, games such as *Minecraft* encourage reading because they do not have extensive tutorials. Readers are forced to figure things out for themselves. Thompson states:

New players immediately set about hunting for info on how it works. That means watching YouTube videos of experts at play, of course, but it also means poring over how-to texts at Minecraft wikis and "walk-through" sites, written by gamers for gamers. Or digging into printed manuals like The Ultimate Player's Guide to Minecraft.[28]

Thompson analyzed some of *The Ultimate Player's Guide to Minecraft* and found that the passages he chose were at an eighth grade to eleventh grade reading level. However, he said that "Games, it seems, can motivate kids to read—and to read way above their level."[29]

Experts such as Hannah Gerber, a researcher at Sam Houston State University, have also found that video games encourage reading. She found that while several tenth grade students only read for ten minutes a day in class, they read seventy minutes at home about their favorite video games. And the material on video games is challenging. In his article, Thompson notes that researcher Constance Steinkuehler at the University of Wisconsin–Madison found that "videogame sites devoted to World of Warcraft, for example, are written at nearly 12th-grade level, with a 2 to 6 percent incidence of 'academic' jargon."[30]

Video games may also help the reading comprehension of children with dyslexia. A study in Italy had half of the participants play nine sessions of an action video game. The other participants played nine sessions of a non-action video game. After playing, researchers tested the participants' reading skills. According to an article by Betsy Isaacson about the study, "Those who had played the action-oriented video game were able to read faster and more accurately, and subsequently did better on other tests measuring attention span." The study also found that "the children who played the action video game for 12 hours saw a larger improvement in reading skills than

Some experts argue that books related to video games help motivate kids to read. Some of these books may tell them about hidden items and codes for the games.

they would have from an average amount of reading during an entire year."[31] By playing a large quantity of video games, students were able to focus longer and read better.

REASONING AND COORDINATION

Spatial reasoning is the ability to visualize objects in three dimensions. One example of spatial reasoning is packing a suitcase. A person must look at the empty space inside the suitcase and visualize whether all of her items will fit. Spatial skills are helpful or even necessary for people working as mechanics, surgeons, and artists, as well as many other careers.

Dr. Gwen Dewar is the founder of ParentingScience.com. She suggests that video games are one of many ways to train young people to gain improved spatial skills. Dewar cites a 2008 study in which college students took weekly mental rotation tests. These measured each participant's ability to mentally turn an object in his mind. In the study, some students were also assigned time to play video games. Some of them played the classic video game *Tetris,* in which the player has to turn differently-shaped blocks to complete rows on the screen, and others played the card game *Solitaire.* The study found that all of the participants improved in their rotation abilities over the course of the studies. However, the students who also played *Tetris* "showed transfer effects, [or] improvement on other related tests of spatial thinking."[32]

Hand-eye coordination is the way that the brain does things that require quick thinking and precise physical movement, such as catching a ball. In a 2016 study, researchers compared people who play action video games at least five hours a week to those who play less than an hour a month. They used a driving simulation in which players needed to drive within the lanes as a crosswind tried to blow the car outside the lanes. The researchers found that "action gamers have better lane-keeping and [hand-eye coordination] than do non–action gamers."[33]

The researchers then had the non-gamers play either action video games or non-action video games for five or ten hours. They saw improvements in the hand-eye coordination of the participants who played action games but did not see any improvements in the participants who played non-action games. The researchers concluded that though different types of action video games, such as driving simulators or first-person shooters, have different effects on the brain, in general they improve a player's hand-eye coordination in as little as five hours.

People who play video games for long periods of time can experience lasting effects from them. But not all of the effects are negative. Some, such as improved hand-eye coordination, can help people in other physical activities.

VIDEO GAMES AND THE BODY

Video games have an effect on the body as well as the brain. Hand-eye coordination requires the body and brain to work together. Video games also improve motor skills, which are the actions that require the use and control of muscles. Dr. Sami Kilic supervises doctors who are training to use robots in surgery. In robotic surgery, the surgeons monitor the actions of a robot on screen. They use hand controllers to control the robot. Kilic discovered that his teenage son, a gamer, had better fine motor skills than the surgeons in training. Fine motor skills involve complicated and precise movements, such as holding a scalpel to make an incision.

Kilic conducted a study to compare the abilities of high school and college age gamers with the abilities of non-gaming surgical residents. The study showed that the people who played video games were better at fine motor skills. It also showed that people who played first-person shooters had increased spatial cognition, or knowledge and awareness of the environment around them.

James C. Rossner Jr. led a similar study. The study found improvements for doctors that played video games before surgery. The researchers concluded that video games improve players' ability to use both hands together, as well as the ability to use their nondominant hand. Psychologist Douglas Gentile was a researcher on the study. Though he supports video games, Gentile warns about playing too much. He said, "There must be some sweet spot in the middle where you get the benefits before you get negative returns."[34]

Finding that "sweet spot" is important because excessive gaming can lead to physical health problems. People who have an addiction to video games as children could experience lifelong repercussions—even if they change their gaming habits later in life.

> **"There must be some sweet spot in the middle where you get the benefits before you get negative returns." [34]**
>
> —Douglas Gentile, psychologist

VIDEO GAME INJURIES

Carpal tunnel syndrome (CTS) is a repetitive motion problem. Actions with the hands that are repeated over and over, such as pressing a button on a game controller, typing on a keyboard, or moving a computer mouse, put pressure on the nerve that runs from the forearm through the wrist and to the hand. CTS can cause tingling or numbness in the fingers and hand, and these symptoms can even run up the entire forearm. This may make the hand weak and unable to grab things.

CTS is a common injury for people who play video games, especially those who play for long periods of time. Writer Ryan Dube found that the combination of his daily activities while writing and gaming in his extra time had detrimental effects on his body. He stated, "I started feeling a strange tingling in the wrist, combined with a numb feeling up the side of my thumb. This eventually evolved into a terrible pain whenever I bent my wrist or my thumb at a certain angle or squeezed my hand."[35] Dube believes that constantly pressing buttons and holding hands at odd angles is what gets many gamers in trouble. He stresses the importance of breaks and stretches during gameplay.

People who have a gaming disorder may experience CTS or other repetitive motion issues. But there are ways to avoid injuries. Some game controllers are more ergonomic than others. This means that they are better suited to a wide variety of people playing them, and they may be better at avoiding stressing or hurting the muscles in the hands and arms. Neil Mansfield is a professor of Design Engineering and Human Factors in London, England. He reviewed several different video game controllers in an article for *Tech Radar*. Mansfield gave the Nintendo 64 controller a five out of ten because of its three handles. He stated, "So at this point here I've got two fingers that are effectively in a stressed position . . . they haven't given me a finger rest at the back here."[36] He also noted that while the shape of the Nintendo 64 controller looks as though it is designed for children, the distance between the A and B buttons is painful for children who have smaller hands. However, Mansfield gave the Nintendo Wiimote and Nunchuck controller an eight out of ten rating. According to the article:

> *The biggest change is the way you hold its two portions, the Wiimote and Nunchuck in separate hands. This means your hands can be nice and wide apart as you use the console, in a neutral 'shoulder-width apart' position. It's also ambidextrous, meaning that it works with left-handed and right-handed people equally as well.*[37]

The choice in video game controllers can help people who play video games for long periods of time avoid injuries. They can also purchase ergonomic equipment designed to avoid stressing the body, including chairs, keyboards, and computer mice. The GTRACING

Holding the hands at odd angles while using the computer or holding a game controller can cause CTS. It can be corrected by wearing braces or having surgery.

gaming office chair has head and lower back support. It also is highly adjustable so people can make it fit their bodies.

Using screens for too long may also damage a person's eyesight. A 2017 study showed that children who use computers or video games for seven hours or more per week tripled their risk for eye problems such as nearsightedness. Continuing to use screens for long periods of time without breaks, as someone may with a video game addiction, may lengthen a person's eyeballs, making the nearsightedness worse.

But some researchers are looking into ways to use video games to improve patients' eyesight. Dr. Mary VanHoy is a neuro-optometrist in Indianapolis, Indiana. She works with patients who have amblyopia, which is a condition where the brain favors one eye over the other. This reduces the vision in that eye. Traditional therapies for amblyopia involve the patient wearing an eyepatch over the stronger eye, which forces the brain to use the weaker eye. But VanHoy uses an Oculus Rift virtual reality (VR) headset instead. According to an article by the American Optometric Association:

> Dr. VanHoy adjusts the contrast or adds partial occlusion to favor the weaker eye, thereby making it work harder in a series of games. Patients generally play one 10-minute session weekly, and in conjunction with other traditional vision therapies. Like a consumer video game, these vision trials feature levels, power-ups and points to engage users, all the while strengthening their eyesight.[38]

Some neuro-optometrists also use Nintendo Wii balance boards for rehabilitation patients. These platforms, designed for use with the Nintendo Wii game *Wii Fit*, measure the distribution of a person's weight in real time, providing instant feedback. The boards help people use multiple body systems at once, and they also give patients the ability to immediately correct their mistakes. A video game habit isn't necessarily an addiction—it may be vision or physical therapy.

SLEEP DEPRIVATION

Stanford Medicine reported that 23 percent of teenagers play video games in the hour before bed. According to a report it issued in 2015, this makes it more difficult to fall asleep even after teens stop playing. Being exposed to lit screens at night tells the part of the brain that controls the sleep/wake cycle that it is not nighttime. "If you ask kids to remove an activity, they would rather not. They would rather give up sleep than an activity," said Nanci Yuan, director of Stanford Children's Health Sleep Center, explaining that teenagers do not self-regulate their sleep well.[39]

Dr. Katherine Morrison says that sleep is key to preventing diseases such as heart diseases and obesity. She conducted a study of children and teens who were in programs for weight management or lipid disorders. The participants wore fitness trackers that monitored the duration and quality of their sleep. The researchers compared that to the participants' video game usage. They found that people who played video games for longer had shorter sleep. "This data shows that gaming addictions can cause numerous health issues in at least a segment of the population," Morrison said.[40] Gaming addictions can have serious repercussions on a person's physical health.

> **"This data shows that gaming addictions can cause numerous health issues in at least a segment of the population."[40]**
>
> *–Dr. Katherine Morrison, researcher*

VIDEO GAME–INDUCED SEIZURES

Epilepsy is a condition in which people have multiple seizures. A seizure is an increase in electrical activity in the brain, often because of a chemical imbalance in the nerve cells. Some people with epilepsy have a greater chance of seizures when exposed to flashing lights. This is known as photosensitive epilepsy, but it has been given another more common name: video game–induced seizures (VGS). These seizures may be caused by flashing lights, pattern sensitivity, and other factors experienced during gameplay. VGS were first recorded in 1981. The first reported case was called "*Space Invaders* epilepsy" after the researchers mixed up that popular game with the game used in the study, *Astro Fighter*.

By 2018, many video game developers and companies had photosensitivity and epilepsy warnings on their websites or within the games themselves. The popular video game streaming website Twitch warns users that, "A very small percentage of individuals may experience epileptic seizures when exposed to certain visual images, including light patterns or flashing lights that may appear in video games or other video content."[41]

Parent Jessica Solodar has a child with photosensitive epilepsy. She started the blog *Seizures from Video Games* to educate other people about the condition. Solodar tested the top games of 2017 using guidelines designed for TV shows to help people avoid seizures. They state that there is more risk for photosensitive seizures if the video game or other form of media has:

- *flash rate greater than 3 [flashes] per second and less than 60*
- *stripes and geometric patterns with high contrast*
- *large areas of very bright ("saturated") red*
- *any of the above problem images taking up more than one quarter of the total screen area*[42]

In 1997, more than 600 children were admitted to a hospital in Japan after watching an episode of the cartoon *Pokémon*. Most of them had photosensitive seizures from a clip where flashing red and blue lights covered the entire screen. Since then, many companies have tried to reduce the risk of photosensitive seizures. However, only four out of GameSpot's 2017 Top 10 Video Games passed the seizure guidelines test. Games such as *The Legend of Zelda: Breath of the Wild* and *Super Mario Odyssey* failed the test. According to Solodar, by passing the test, games such as *Horizon Zero Dawn* are "unlikely to provoke seizures in 97% of people with photosensitive epilepsy."[43]

People may not know they have epilepsy or photosensitivity. In 2016, a popular E-Sports player known as Lothar had a seizure while livestreaming the game Hearthstone on Twitch. As of 2018 he had not reported any other photosensitive seizures. People can have photosensitive seizures without being diagnosed with epilepsy. A study in England showed that 1.3 percent of school children had "abnormal responses to strobe lights."[44] Some people with addictions to video games may ignore warnings intended to reduce the chance of seizures, such as taking a break every hour or playing on a small screen.

Playing video games for long periods of time has both positive and negative effects on the brain and body. Potential benefits include improved hand-eye coordination. Potential downsides include the risk of seizures as well as worsened eyesight. But video games do not just affect one person's brain and body. An addiction to video games can have profound effects on local communities as well as the world. As video games become more popular and more widespread, the solutions for addiction may become much larger and more comprehensive.

CHAPTER 3

HOW DOES VIDEO GAME ADDICTION AFFECT **OUR WORLD?**

A 2017 report from market research company Newzoo stated that the worldwide video game market was expected to generate $108.9 billion dollars that year. The report also noted that there are 2.2 billion people around the world who play video games. As these numbers continue to rise, video game addiction may become a problem that affects the entire world.

Ches Hall, a NASA engineer and the creator of a video game podcast, says that people shouldn't dismiss the idea of video game addiction. He continues, "After all, many game publishers are calling on psychologists and the experience of casinos to figure out how to draw players in for longer periods of time while offering shallow content."[45] Some countries are trying to stop the problem with regulations on video game sales or playing hours. Others are establishing treatment programs for people with addiction. But some people believe that video game addiction is not the problem. Many people have careers playing or developing video games for a living. Some experts argue that video games are not the problem, and that excessive video game playing is merely a symptom of other issues.

The Nintendo Game Boy helped launch gaming on the go. Some experts believe that this has led people to become more addicted to video games.

LOOT BOXES

In 2018, legislators in Hawaii, Washington, Minnesota, and Illinois introduced bills on the subject of video game loot boxes. Loot boxes are features of video game where players can purchase boxes in-game that contains a random special item or power-up. Some people are concerned that loot boxes are a form of gambling. Players spend money not knowing which prize they will receive in a game of chance. Senator Kevin Ranker in Washington requested that the state's gambling commission decide whether loot boxes count as gambling. In Hawaii, Representative Chris Lee proposed four bills to limit the age of people who could buy loot boxes and require game companies to reveal the odds of finding particular items in loot boxes.

The Entertainment Software Rating Board (ESRB), a group established by the gaming industry, believes that loot boxes are closer to collectible trading cards rather than gambling. It states, "While there's an element of chance in these mechanics, the player is always guaranteed to receive in-game content (even if the player unfortunately receives something they don't want)."[46] However, writer Ellen McGrody believes that many people feel about their loot box purchases like they might feel about a gambling addiction. She writes, "There are people, probably more than we think, who have been seriously impacted by the consequences of impulsive spending in games."[47]

McGrody notes that many people she interviewed felt embarrassed or ashamed of their loot box purchases, often regretting them the next day. This led to tension with family and friends. But in the moment, the allure of loot boxes felt addictive. One player, who spent several hundred dollars on loot boxes in games such as *Overwatch,* reported that "I felt compelled to spend on loot boxes every time a limited time event started so I wouldn't miss out. It warped my whole perception of the game into short periods of anxiety and stress where I had to spend money or play constantly [in] the hope of not missing out."[48] Other players reported problems with gambling

> **"I felt compelled to spend on loot boxes every time a limited time event started so I wouldn't miss out. It warped my whole perception of the game into short periods of anxiety and stress where I had to spend money or play constantly [in] the hope of not missing out."** [48]
>
> *–anonymous* Overwatch *player*

or online shopping addictions in the past which easily turned into loot box addictions.

By the end of the 2018 legislative session, none of the loot box bills advanced in state legislatures. But people have not stopped trying to regulate video games. Representative Lee noted that he had been talking about the issue with representatives from thirty other states.

GAMING RULES IN OTHER COUNTRIES

In 2017, China announced that it would pass laws to regulate boot camp treatment centers such as the Addiction Treatment Center in Shandong, China. Some of these treatment centers were infamous for using electroshock therapy on their patients with online gaming addictions. If passed, the laws would regulate the physical punishments that these centers used. They would also require restrictions on the amount of time that people could use internet cafés and online games. Many people believe this is a step in the right direction for treating gaming addiction. Dr. Tao Ran, the director of the Internet Addiction Clinic in Beijing, states, "It's a very important move for protecting young children."[49] However, he added that it would not be very easy to enforce these laws around the country.

South Korea also has boot camp treatment centers for people with gaming addictions. Researcher Christian Montag conducted a study that showed that the "highest prevalence of 'problematic internet use' worldwide has been in Asia," with South Korea having the "highest rate of problematic internet use."[50] One infamous case of video game addiction happened in 2010, when a South Korean couple played video games for so long and so often that their baby starved to death. In 2011, the South Korean government passed the Youth Protection Revision Act, which is commonly called the

OVERWATCH LOOT BOXES IN CHINA

Blizzard Entertainment, the developers of *Overwatch*, hid the likelihood of winning various prizes in loot boxes. But in May 2017, the Chinese government passed regulations that forced Blizzard to disclose the rates for the loot boxes in China. According to the Chinese version of the *Overwatch* site, each loot box has at least one rare item. The chance of finding an epic item is 1 out of 5.5 loot boxes. Legendary items are in 1 out of every 13.5 boxes. While there are free ways to earn loot boxes, most people purchase them.

However, in June 2017, Blizzard decided to sell the in-game currency to players in China directly to get around China's gambling regulation laws. Before, the currency could only be found in the loot boxes themselves. Players can use the currency for special skins, or styles for their characters, as well as legendary items. However, journalist Allegra Frank says, "It will take quite a bit of cash for Chinese players to buy that legendary skin they want, though: Those cost 3,000 credits." That could be approximately $875 US dollars per skin.

Allegra Frank, "Overwatch Players Can Start Buying Credits in China," Polygon, June 5, 2017. www.polygon.com.

Cinderella Law. This law restricts online computer gaming access to minors under the age of sixteen between midnight and 6:00 am. However, in 2014 the law was amended to allow parents to permit their children to play games after midnight. While the law was still in effect as of 2018, research has shown that the law has not had any lasting effects on internet addiction. The law also does not affect console games or mobile games.

While other countries in Europe such as the United Kingdom have not cracked down on loot boxes, in 2018, Belgium banned loot boxes entirely, citing that loot boxes are "in violation of gambling legislation" in the country.[51] Belgium instituted a fine of $931 million for developers that do not remove loot boxes from their games. One anonymous internet user stated that the law from Belgium is a great way to "avoid taking advantage of kids with fancy and shiny in-your-face computer graphics and images."[52] It may also be useful in helping people with video game addictions. However, other people are worried that rather than following these new rules, game companies may simply decide not to sell their video games in Belgium.

SCREEN TIME

Parents can limit daily screen time to help children with video game addiction, or they may decide to allow gaming only on the weekend. One Iowa family reported locking up laptops, iPods, and tablets in a backpack before bed to keep their eleven-year-old son from playing games through the night. The father, Scott Timm, was furious when he discovered that his son had cut a hole in the backpack's side to sneak out electronic devices. Timm explained, "He'd sneak electronics, so he'd lose the privilege, but then he would sneak it again, then lose more time. It was a constant struggle."[53]

The Timms are not alone. Even major leaders of the technology industry, such as Bill Gates, founder of Microsoft, and Steve Jobs, cofounder of Apple, limited the use of technology for their children. In 2007, Gates stated that he limited screen time after his daughter became too attached to video games. In 2011, Jobs said that his children were not allowed to use an iPad because they limited technology in the home. Joe Clement and Matt Miles, authors of *Screen Schooled: Two Veteran Teachers Expose How Technology Overuse Is Making Our Kids Dumber*, ask: "What is it these wealthy tech executives know about their own products that their consumers don't?"[54]

However, many people argue that a no-tech lifestyle is impossible today. Dr. Peter Gray states, "Our limiting kids' computer time would be like hunter-gatherer adults limiting their kids' bow-and-arrow time."[55] Writer Nanea Hoffman also considers technology a tool. In an article in the *Washington Post*, Hoffman states that she does not have any screen time limitations for her children. Instead, children are free to use technology after they have done their chores, finished homework, and fulfilled family obligations. The flexibility works for her family. She states, "There are days when no screen time happens if homework and activities fill up the schedule, and there are weekends when our children retreat to a bedroom for a Netflix-palooza, emerging mostly for meals and snacks."[56]

Hoffman does not want her children to be afraid of or mystified by technology. She adds: "For my children, technology . . . doesn't control or oppress them. It's a tool. . . . It's not a big deal. Screen time, for us, is still time spent together."[57]

> **"For my children, technology . . . doesn't control or oppress them. It's a tool. . . . It's not a big deal. Screen time, for us, is still time spent together."[57]**
>
> —*Nanea Hoffman, writer*

SOCIALIZATION

The Entertainment Software Association (ESA) found that 53 percent of the most frequent gamers play MMOs. MMOs such as *World of Warcraft* are often subject to negative stereotypes, with people

48

assuming that they suck players into spending more time in a digital world than the real world. Because players work with others online to battle enemies and conquer dungeons, there is pressure to play for many hours at a time at specific hours every week. The authors of *Glued to Games* wrote, "With more than 10 million players as of 2018, *World of Warcraft* alone has many parents and spouses 'worried about Warcraft,' as they watch family members disappear into this virtual world—and many others like it—for large portions of each day."[58]

While extreme cases of people addicted to MMOs exist, many people enjoy the socialization aspect of such games. According to Dr. Peter Gray, "Making friends within the game requires essentially the same skills as making friends in the real world. You can't be rude."[59] Players in MMOs must work cooperatively to battle enemies and defeat opponents. Those who do not get along with others cannot progress in the story of the game. Gray notes that they may end up on a block list instead of a friends list.

In fact, some people can even find romantic partners through cooperative video games. One user who goes by the name Bliss online met her boyfriend while playing *Minecraft*. The two did not meet in person until three years into their relationship, when her boyfriend flew from Germany to her hometown in Florida. Bliss says that people do not typically go looking for online relationships while playing video games, but that they just happen over time.

Dr. Vivian Zayas, the director of the Personality, Attachment, and Control Laboratory at Cornell University, has an answer to the phenomenon of finding partners while playing video games. She compares online dating sites to shopping for a partner, "but playing these games and chatting, the mentality is more organic, like in a normal social network."[60] Playing video games online with teammates all over the world gives people a chance to expand their social circles. While critics of video games state that they create people who have lost their abilities to socialize, games have similar structures to real-world social situations. Some games have guilds where people with similar interests can gather to chat or battle enemies. Gray states:

Guilds generally have structures that are similar to companies in the real world, with leaders, executive boards, and even recruitment personnel. . . . In fact, a study commissioned by the IBM Corporation concluded that the leadership skills exercised within MMORPGs are essentially the same as those required to run a modern company.[61]

GAMES IN HOSPITALS

The organization Gamers Outreach strives to help children in hospitals feel less lonely through the use of video games. The group has worked with more than forty hospitals in the United States and Canada to provide Gamers Outreach Karts, or GO Karts, for children who cannot leave their beds. These GO Karts are portable video game kiosks. "Our intent is to inspire and heal patients through interactive play," say the organizers of Gamers Outreach.[62]

Gamers Outreach also created the Player 2 program, through which gamers volunteer to help manage the equipment and give tech support, plus play the games with patients. "A lot of hospitals and fundraising organizations [are] concerned with treatment and research, which is priority, but there's not a lot of investment in quality of life or entertainment," said Gamers Outreach founder Zach Wigal. "That's where we come in, as a nonprofit, and say we think this is valuable."[63]

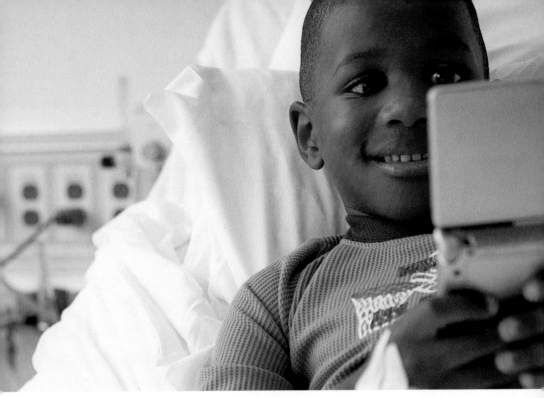

Programs such as Gamers Outreach bring video games to hospital patients. This can help them feel less isolated and alone.

GAMING AND MENTAL DISORDERS

Some people may have medical conditions or disabilities that make it easier to communicate in a virtual world. People with agoraphobia, a fear that may involve never leaving the house, may be able to socialize safely through video games. People with depression or anxiety can feel connected to others while playing games. Research conducted in Taiwan showed that people with social anxiety decrease their level of anxiety by playing MMORPGs. Players with social anxiety can use these games to talk about their real-life problems with in-game friends much the way most people talk to their friends in person or over the phone. "MMORPGs also provide interactive elements to encourage players with whom it may not be easy to talk in face-to-face situations, interact with others, and seek social connections," said

51

the study's authors.[64] This in turn could help relieve the loneliness and depression that some people with social phobias experience.

According to a study at the University of Missouri, "children with [autism spectrum disorder (ASD)] spent much more time playing video games than typically developing children, and they are much more likely to develop problematic or addictive patterns of video game play."[65] The study's lead researcher, Dr. Micah Mazurek, looked at 202 children with ASD and their 179 siblings who did not have ASD. Mazurek found that the participants with ASD spent more time playing video games than checking social media or playing outside. However, Mazurek notes, "Children with ASD may be attracted to video games because they can be rewarding, visually engaging and do not require face-to-face communication or social interaction."[66] Rather than being an addiction, video games and other forms of technology may be a different way for people to communicate.

WORK AND SCHOOL

Melanie Hempe is the founder of Families Managing Media, an organization that helps families create a balanced digital lifestyle. According to Hempe, video game overuse is one of the primary reasons why young men drop out of or fail college. She points out that "85 [percent] of college men are game players, and one in eight develops addiction patterns."[67] Some college orientations even warn parents about the dangers of video game use once their children go to college. However, children aren't the only ones affected by video game addiction. Adults can develop addictions to video games as well. One person in the online support group Game Quitters shared his true story. He had been addicted to gaming since he was a child, but didn't seek help until it impacted his marriage and family.

He switched shifts at work so he would have more time to play video games before his wife and children woke up. He continued, "What ran through my mind was having the ability to stay up past my kids bedtime before I had to leave to spend time on gaming, and have the following morning before the kids and wife woke up to game as well."[68]

Though video game use is worrying people around the world, digital technology has never been more accessible for kids. According to a 2016 survey of digital trends, the average age of a child in the United States when he or she first gets a cell phone—another tool that allows easy access to games—is ten years old. Tablets are often viewed as educational toys as well as entertainment.

> "What ran through my mind was having the ability to stay up past my kids bedtime before I had to leave to spend time on gaming, and have the following morning before the kids and wife woke up to game as well." [68]
>
> —anonymous Game Quitters member

To many experts, video games are a potent learning tool for education. In 1977, the computer game *The Oregon Trail* was released in classrooms across Minnesota by the Minnesota Educational Computing Consortium (MECC). The game had been programmed a few years earlier by student teachers Don Rawitsch, Bill Heinemann, and Paul Dillenberger to teach students about the history of settlers moving west in the 1800s. When Rawitsch went to work at MECC, he typed up the game and made it available across the state. In the

1980s, the game became popular around the country for teaching students about the Oregon Trail and the various ways settlers could survive, such as by hunting and rationing their supplies, or die, such as by getting bitten by a snake or contracting dysentery.

There are many views on why games work in education. In *The Game Believes in You*, writer Greg Toppo puts it simply, "Real learning, games showed, was always associated with pleasure and is ultimately a form of play."[69] Gamers may have to memorize information and apply that knowledge to win the game. For example, Pokémon players are more successful if they know the strengths and weaknesses for more than 750 fictional creatures. People can also learn about history, biology, and music. Educational games engage the players' interest in learning everything they can about a game world to convey information about history, math, science, and other topics.

Additionally, video games can help people practice persistence. According to professor Dr. LaShera McElhany, "When faced with problems in real-life, we can become anxious, overwhelmed, and feel like giving up. In gaming worlds when confronted with a problem or obstacle, the player is motivated to persist until the problem is solved. Then, the player advances to the next level."[70]

> **"When faced with problems in real-life, we can become anxious, overwhelmed, and feel like giving up. In gaming worlds when confronted with a problem or obstacle, the player is motivated to persist until the problem is solved."** [70]
>
> *–Dr. LaShera McElhany, professor*

CAREERS IN GAMING

Several decades ago the only jobs in the video game industry were development positions such as artists, programmers, and marketers. Now people can earn money playing video games online for an audience. Streaming services such as Twitch and YouTube Gaming let gamers make money by playing games. In 2017 Twitch had more than two million unique streamers every month and 27,000 Partners who can make money from their livestreams of video games. There are more than fifteen million unique visitors to Twitch every day. Streamers on YouTube Gaming can monetize their channels so they get paid for the ads that people watch during their videos.

Some people even play video games professionally. Gamers all over the world compete in E-Sports tournaments for large prizes. In 2017, the *Dota 2* championships at The International tournament had a prize pool of almost $25 million. The publisher of *Fortnite*, Epic Games, pledged to provide $100 million to fund E-Sports tournaments during the 2018–2019 season. E-Sports players and teams can make money from events, tournaments, and company sponsorships. Team Liquid has won millions of dollars from E-Sports tournaments and sponsorships. As of 2018, the team had earned more than $18.2 million in prize money. People who earn a living through streaming or competitive play are likely to spend hours each day playing games. For them, these extended play sessions are a career.

Video games have entered almost every area of society from the individual to the world. With that comes the potential for over-use or addiction. In the future, legislation, recovery and treatment options, and prevention methods may help people better understand video game addiction.

THE FUTURE OF VIDEO
GAME ADDICTION

Not everyone looks at the brightly projected future of video games as a problem. "I think video games are going to completely take over storytelling in our society," says Guillermo del Toro, writer and director of films including *Pan's Labyrinth* and *The Shape of Water*. "Video games are not a fad. They are absolutely a narrative form."[71]

It is difficult to imagine a world in which technology and video games would cease to exist. Games exist on every piece of technology people own, from phones to tablets to computers. People are able to access video games wherever they are. As the popularity of games spreads, there are concerns that video game addiction will also rise. Mental health professionals across the globe are finding new ways to treat video game addiction, as well as using video games to treat other mental illnesses.

MORE GAMERS CAUSING MORE ADDICTION

As more and more people are taking up video games as a hobby, spending on video games is also skyrocketing. In 2010, $17.5 billion was spent on games in the United States; in 2016, that figure zoomed

READY PLAYER ONE: BALANCING A VIRTUAL AND REAL LIFE

The science fiction adventure film *Ready Player One* hit theaters in 2018. Based on the novel of the same name, the film depicts a future world in which cities have become slums so horrible that residents escape to a digital world called the OASIS. The story's hero, Wade, fights to secure this digital world from the hands of a greedy corporation. Along the way, he learns that the true prize is life outside the OASIS. In an interview with *Collider*, the director Steven Spielberg said:

I think anybody who read the book, who was connected, at all, with the movie industry, would have loved to have made this into a movie. . . . It was just a matter of trying to figure out how to tell the story . . . and, at the same time, make it a cautionary tale about leaving us the choice of where we want to exist. Do we want to exist in reality, or do we want to exist in an escapist universe? Those themes were so profound for me.

Quoted in Christina Radish, "Steven Spielberg on 'Ready Player One' and Why He'll Never Rework His Own Movies Again," Collider, March 28, 2018. www.collider.com

to $24.5 billion. As of 2016, 2.5 billion people played video games. By 2020, global video game sales are expected to leap to $90 billion. This is up from $78.6 billion in 2017. With all of this growth expected in so short a time, some experts fear addictions will follow.

Part of the growth in video game sales follows a growth in access to technology in schools. Many parents and teachers see one-to-one technology in classrooms, where every student is given a laptop or tablet, as good thing. Kardaras, however, sees the tech-heavy classrooms as a hurdle for students. In a *Time* article, he says:

I've worked with over a thousand teens in the past 15 years and have observed that students who have been raised on a high-tech diet . . . appear to struggle more with attention and focus . . . that appears to be a direct byproduct of their digital immersion.[72]

Giving students so much access to technology has been shown to have significant psychological effects. Kardaras adds that "over two hundred peer-reviewed studies point to screen time correlating to increased ADHD, screen addiction, increased aggression, depression, anxiety and even psychosis."[73]

However, educators feel that one-to-one technology helps more than hurts students. Teachers point to an increased ability for students to access a wide variety of resources. McGraw-Hill Education, a major textbook publisher, cites an increase in student-teacher communication and peer collaboration. Trends in sales of one-to-one technology are not declining either. In 2016, 54 percent of K–12 classrooms in the United States used some form of one-to-one technology. The data trends point to continued growth for one-to-one technology in the future.

> **"Students who have been raised on a high-tech diet not only appear to struggle more with attention and focus . . . that appears to be a direct byproduct of their digital immersion."** [72]
>
> *–Dr. Nicholas Kardaras, psychologist*

UNDERSTANDING THROUGH RESEARCH

In 2017, the University of Connecticut School of Medicine began a two-year study to help determine if the APA should include IGD

Some experts argue that technology in schools contributes to addiction. Others believe it allows for better education and collaboration.

as a true mental health disorder. This would make it a diagnosis that could be covered by insurance. The research is funded by the NIH and focuses on problematic gamers ages thirteen to eighteen. Researchers planned to split the study group in two, testing typical treatments available against treatments designed by the APA.

This is long overdue in the eyes of some scientists. As far back as 1999, Dr. David Greenfield, founder of the Center for Internet and Technology Addiction, warned of compulsive usage. He continues to talk about how it remains a problem today. "There was no high-speed internet, no Wi-Fi, no laptops or tablets, no smartphones, and it was already an issue," he said. "But now, because we have greater ease of access and it's easier to pick and click and have that automatic intoxication of response, it's more addictive."[74]

Experts recognize that some people develop problematic habits related to video games. However, there is little consensus over whether IGD is an addiction, or something else.. The condition has been added to the *DSM* as a disorder that needs more research. But video game addiction does not have a standard diagnosis yet. This is due to the varying opinions of professionals in the field.

Some professionals say it is a co-occurring disorder, meaning that it shows up with another illness such as depression or anxiety. Doctors prescribe medication to treat the depression or anxiety, and video game usage decreases. Other experts claim it is an impulse control disorder. More research is needed in order to really understand the nature of video game addiction and the way it impacts people's lives.

VIDEO GAMES AS THERAPY

Some therapists around the world are beginning to use video games in their practices. Therapists see far-reaching effects of video games in their clients' lives, and they use video games not only for therapeutic practices but also as a way to make connections with their clients.

A therapists' rapport, or relationship, with their client is very important in the counseling process. Asking a young person whether he plays video games can be a good way to find out more information and also get the client to talk more freely. One therapist said,

[I] once conducted a session where [I] and the client were playing a racing videogame in session. The client commented that it reminded him of when he used to play videogames with his father. [I] asked the client what he would tell his father if he was also playing the racing game at that moment. The client talked about his sadness and said that he would tell his father that he misses him.[75]

Video games are not new to therapy, but data from case studies proving the use of games is beneficial has been limited. Some have been used to teach youth about consequences of their actions or to deal with aggressive behavior in young people. Some researchers began to focus on evaluating cognitive skills, how easily subjects became frustrated, and even understanding how a child's style of play may offer clues to the root of their problems in psychotherapy.

There are other ways video games are being used therapeutically, including for traumatic brain injury. Weekly, one-hour games in a group session improve self-awareness, social skills, and other behaviors. For those struggling with bulimia, an eating disorder that can be life threatening, therapy that involved video games was found to help clients regulate their emotions, which is often a problem for those with the eating disorder. People diagnosed with attention deficit hyperactivity disorder (ADHD) are more susceptible to video game addiction, so one company designed a video game to help them. Akili Interactive Labs designed an action game that, in a study of 348 children, was shown to improve their attention and ability to control their inhibitions.

VR gaming technology is also being introduced to treat

> **"[I] once conducted a session where [I] and the client were playing a racing videogame in session. The client commented that it reminded him of when he used to play videogames with his father."** [75]
>
> *–anonymous therapist*

a variety of illnesses. The Oculus Rift VR headset was introduced to consumers in 2016. There are some experts that fear this reality-shifting technology could create a whole new level of addiction in adolescents and adults. One researcher, Jeremy Bailenson, says, "the brain cannot tell the difference between an actual or virtual experience."[76] This leads to the possibility of a collection of false memories.

However some therapists are seeing VR as an important opportunity to try new methods with clients. Dr. Patrick Bordnick at the University of Houston has recognized ways in which VR might be used to help treat substance abuse disorders such as alcoholism and nicotine addictions. Many therapists use cue-reactivity treatment for clients with addictions. Cue-reactivity uses a cue, such as a photo of a cigarette, to trigger a reaction. The goal of cue-reactivity therapy is to teach coping skills that clients can take into the real world. But Dr. Bordnick says there are limitations to traditional cue-reactivity treatments. The biggest issue is that clients know they are in a lab environment. VR cue-reactivity therapies shift that perception. Artists are able to create simulations of actual environments the clients might be exposed to, such as a bar, the outside of a coffee shop, or a party. In some cases, therapists go as far as simulating the smell of cigarette smoke to trigger a craving. More studies are needed, but preliminary research shows that VR may be helpful in assisting other therapeutic forms.

A study led by Bordnick used forty-six smokers in a ten-week program. One group was given VR cue-reactivity treatments as well as nicotine replacement therapy such as gum or patches. The other group received only nicotine replacement therapy. At the end of the study the VR group showed lower smoking rates and cravings.

VR may soon have a use in therapy to help patients learn to cope with specific triggers. For example, people could use VR simulations to help them stop smoking.

LIVING A SEDENTARY LIFESTYLE

Playing games for many hours per week leads to a sedentary lifestyle. People who display addictive behaviors resist doing anything else because it doesn't register as more pleasurable than gaming. This can lead to medical conditions such as lower bone density. Having a lower bone density means that bones are more likely to break. According to Dr. Katya Herman:

> Childhood and adolescence is when we are building the
> most bone in our body. So to negatively affect that at a lower
> peak bone density, you've got less room to move at older

adulthood, until you hit the zone of being osteoporotic and in
danger of easily fracturing.[77]

A study by the University of British Columbia showed that only
9 percent of girls and 43 percent of boys were physically active for the
recommended sixty minutes per day. This could negatively affect their
bone density. Herman recommends, "Instead of sitting for three hours
straight, or six hours straight, or an entire day on a weekend playing
video games, get up a few times an hour. Take a break, go for a walk
around, and come back for the sedentary pursuit."[78]

One option may be "exergaming," or using active video games
for the Xbox Kinect and Nintendo Wii. Dr. Amanda Staiano studied
forty-one overweight or obese teenage girls in Baton Rouge,
Louisiana. She had them play dancing games using the Xbox Kinect
for three hours a week over the course of three months. Staiano noted
that the participants' bone density increased during the study. The
video games increased bone density at a crucial time for the participants.
After adolescence, bone density starts to decrease.

Other scientists caution against using video games as the only source of
exercise. Dr. Hollie Raynor, director of the

> **"Instead of sitting for three hours straight, or six hours straight, or an entire day on a weekend playing video games, get up a few times an hour." [78]**
>
> –Dr. Katya Herman, professor

University of Tennessee's Healthy Eating and Activity Laboratory, says, "We're not saying video games should replace outdoor play, but there are better choices people can make when choosing the types of video games for their children."[79] One study done in 2012 showed no difference in activity levels between kids who played active games and kids who played inactive games. Accelerometers, devices that measure motion, showed that both groups were active for twenty-five to twenty-eight minutes per day. The Centers for Disease Control and Prevention (CDC) recommends that kids get at least sixty minutes of physical activity per day. This means that even with the choice of active games, the participants in the 2012 study were not getting enough exercise.

TREATMENT AND PREVENTION

Though the United States has lagged in doing research and taking gaming problems seriously, other countries such as China and South Korea have been more proactive. In China, there are 300 treatment centers designed to help those who are addicted to gaming; in comparison, the United States only has a handful of treatment centers.

One of these US treatment centers is the reSTART center in Seattle, Washington. The center has a wide variety of treatment plans for clients. Many of reSTART's programs are residential, meaning that clients live with other program participants. The center uses techniques such as group therapy, nutrition coaching, weekend adventures, and personalized clinical plans, as well as other practices. The program notes in its mission that:

By providing opportunities for engagement in a variety of areas
from social, recreational, academic, work, and community

People with video game addiction can participate in group therapy. This therapy allows people to share their stories and receive advice from others.

events, to environmental, spiritual and humanitarian arenas, people develop the capacity to maintain change, and overcome obstacles.[80]

Many people who suffer from IGD find it helpful to be in groups with other people struggling with the same problems. One client from reSTART says, "It was immensely helpful to struggle alongside other guys in similar situations. We learned from each other's struggles and encouraged each other to press on."[81] Participants in the program create a community outside of the video games and have a network of support as they continue their healing.

A history of empirical studies shows that reSTART's methods work. But professionals such as the authors of *Grand Theft Childhood*, Kutner and Olson, recommend careful evaluation of any facility before signing up. "What are needed, of course, are well-designed scientific studies of both the video game addiction diagnosis and various treatments."[82]

Another option is wilderness therapy, or Outdoor Behavioral Counseling. It is a prescribed therapy treatment that sends clients to adventure programs. These programs are led and monitored by mental health professionals. The goal of this is not to separate the addicted person from technology—though that is one aspect of the program—but to focus on teaching survival skills, team building, and achieving goals in order to build self-confidence. This works to alleviate some of the anxiety and depression that are thought to be some of the common underlying disorders that trigger video game overuse. This therapy also removes emotional escapes so participants must learn to face and handle their emotions.

> "What are needed, of course, are well-designed scientific studies of both the video game addiction diagnosis and various treatments." [82]
>
> —Dr. Lawrence Kutner and Dr. Cheryl K. Olson, authors of Grand Theft Childhood

Video games and technology are best when players find a balance between gaming and other ways to have fun. Friends can spend time together in the digital world and in the real world.

In the United States alone there are more than one hundred wilderness therapy programs. Each year, it is estimated that they serve 10,000 clients. More than 80 percent of participants in outdoor behavioral programs reported they were doing better one year after the end of the program.

For people who do not have access to these therapies, there are still strategies that may help them. For children who are problematic players, experts recommend parents either remove the games from the home or carefully limit and monitor gameplay in the home. Dr. David Greenfield suggests parents also model the behavior they want to see in their children. Additionally, it is recommended that both adolescents and adults turn off technology at least one hour before bed. Whichever treatment plan a family chooses, replacing the game time with quality family time and activities is recommended. Dr. Greenfield suggests making a "real-time 100" list of activities parents and children can do together that don't involve screens.[83]

Even Apple is making an effort to assist in helping people spend less time on their phones. In 2018, it announced that the newest version of its iOS operating system would include tools to help consumers check their phone less often. The software update let users see a breakdown of how much they use their phones and even how much time they spend in certain apps. It also lets users know which apps are sending the most notifications.

Parents will also be able to monitor their kids' phone use. Through the Family Sharing app, parents can set use limits for their kids' phones. Once the limit has been reached, the app kicks users out. Parents can also access tips about phone use on Apple's website.

Video games and the technology that makes them so readily available aren't going away. There is consistent growth in the gaming industry, and video games are reaching children at younger and younger ages. An increase in video game addiction can be expected in the future, especially as doctors learn more about this condition and how to accurately recognize it in adolescents and adults.

It is important to recognize that, like so much in life, finding balance is important. Striking that balance is the responsibility of a gamer. In the case of young gamers, parents can help them find that balance. There are many benefits that can be found in video games, but spending too much time in front of a screen can cause significant physical and mental health issues.

SOURCE NOTES

INTRODUCTION: ADDICTION AND RECOVERY

1. Quoted in Sarah Klein, "I Went to Rehab for My Technology Addiction," *Prevention*, October 19, 2016. www.prevention.com.

2. Quoted in Klein, "I Went to Rehab for My Technology Addiction."

3. Quoted in Tiffany Hsu, "Video Game Addiction Tries to Move from Basement to Doctor's Office," *New York Times*, June 17, 2018. www.nytimes.com.

4. Quoted in Tamara Lush, "At War with World of Warcraft: An Addict Tells His Story," *Guardian*, August 29, 2011. www.theguardian.com.

5. Quoted in Barbara Booth, "Internet Addiction Is Sweeping America, Affecting Millions," *CNBC*, August 29, 2017. www.cnbc.com.

CHAPTER 1: WHAT IS VIDEO GAME ADDICTION?

6. Quoted in Stephanie A. Sarkis, "Internet Gaming Disorder in DSM-5," *Psychology Today*, July 18, 2014. www.psychologytoday.com.

7. Nicholas Kardaras, "It's 'Digital Heroin': How Screens Turn Kids into Psychotic Junkies," *New York Post*, August 27, 2016. www.nypost.com.

8. Kardaras, "It's 'Digital Heroin.'"

9. Quoted in Cecilia D'Anastasio, "Experts Have a New Reason to Debate Whether 'Gaming Disorder' Is Real," *Kotaku*, December 27, 2017. www.kotaku.com.

10. Peter Gray, "Sense and Nonsense About Video Game Addiction," *Psychology Today*, March 11, 2018. www.psychologytoday.com.

11. Gray, "Sense and Nonsense About Video Game Addiction."

12. Jolyon Jenkins, "Should Parents Ever Worry About Minecraft?" *BBC News*, March 30, 2015. www.bbc.com.

13. Ferris Jabr, "How the Brain Gets Addicted to Gambling," *Scientific American*, November 1, 2013. www.scientificamerican.com.

14. Lawrence Kutner and Cheryl K. Olson, *Grand Theft Childhood*. New York: Simon and Shuster, 2008, p. 157.

15. Scott Rigby and Richard M. Ryan, *Glued to Games: How Video Games Draw Us In and Hold Us Spellbound*. Santa Barbara, CA: Praeger, 2011, p. 101.

16. Quoted in D'Anastasio, "Experts Have a New Reason to Debate."

17. Quoted in D'Anastasio, "Experts Have a New Reason to Debate."

CHAPTER 2: HOW DOES VIDEO GAME ADDICTION AFFECT THE BRAIN AND BODY?

18. "Drugs, Brains, and Behavior: The Science of Addiction," *National Institute on Drug Abuse*, June 2018. www.drugabuse.gov.

19. "Drugs, Brains, and Behavior: The Science of Addiction."

20. "Drugs, Brains, and Behavior: The Science of Addiction."

21. Kardaras, "It's 'Digital Heroin.'"

22. Jack Flanagan, "The Psychology of Video Game Addiction," *The Week*, February 6, 2014. www.theweek.com.

23. Gray, "Sense and Nonsense about Video Game Addiction."

24. Rigby and Ryan, *Glued to Games*, p. 102.

25. Rigby and Ryan, *Glued to Games*, p. 103.

26. Rigby and Ryan, *Glued to Games*, p. 103.

27. Quoted in Jamie Madigan, "The Zeigarnik Effect and Quest Logs," *Psychology of Games*, March 6, 2013. www.psychologyofgames.com.

28. Clive Thompson, "How Videogames Like Minecraft Actually Help Kids Learn to Read," *Wired*, October 9, 2014. www.wired.com.

29. Thompson, "How Videogames Like Minecraft Actually Help Kids Learn to Read."

30. Thompson, "How Videogames Like Minecraft Actually Help Kids Learn to Read."

31. Betty Isaacson, "Video Games May Improve Reading Skills in Children with Dyslexia: Study," *Huffington Post*, March 8, 2013. www.huffingtonpost.com.

32. Gwen Dewar, "10 Tips for Improving Spatial Skills in Children and Teens," *Parentingscience.com*, 2016. www.parentingscience.com.

33. Li Li, Rongrong Chen, and Jing Chen, "Playing Action Video Games Improves Visuomotor Control," *Psychological Science*, July 8, 2016, pp. 1092–1108.

34. Quoted in Klint Finley, "How Videogames Could Help Train the Next Generation of Robotic Surgeons," *Wired*, December 11, 2012. www.wired.com.

35. Ryan Dube, "5 Dangerous Gaming Injuries and How to Avoid Them," *MakeUseOf*, September 18, 2013. www.makeuseof.com.

36. Quoted in Jon Porter, "The Ultimate Gaming Controllers for Comfort: An Expert's Guide," *TechRadar*, March 9, 2017. www.techradar.com.

37. Porter, "The Ultimate Gaming Controllers for Comfort."

38. American Optometric Association, "Video-Game Vision Therapy," *AOA Focus*, April 2016. www.aoa.org.

39. Quoted in Ruthann Richter, "Go to Bed," *Stanford Medicine*, Fall 2015. www.stanmed.stanford.edu.

40. Quoted in McMaster University, "Videogame Addiction Leads to Sleep Loss, Obesity, and Cardiovascular Risk in Some Gamers," *ScienceDaily*, May 9, 2016. www.sciencedaily.com.

41. "Photosensitive Seizure Warning," *Twitch*, n.d. www.twitch.tv.

42. Jessica Solodar, "Seizures from 2017's Best Video Games," *Seizures from Video Games*, February 15, 2018. www.videogameseizures.wordpress.com.

43. Solodar, "Seizures from 2017's Best Video Games."

44. Giussepe Erba, "Shedding Light on Photosensitivity, One of Epilepsy's Most Complex Conditions," *Epilepsy Foundation*, n.d. www.epilepsy.com.

45. Quoted in Quora, "How Big of a Problem Is Video Game Addiction?" *Forbes*, August 11, 2017. www.forbes.com.

CHAPTER 3: HOW DOES VIDEO GAME ADDICTION AFFECT OUR WORLD?

46. Quoted in David Lumb, "Can Legislation Fix Gaming's Loot Box Problem?" *Engadget*, February 24, 2018. www.engadget.com.

47. Ellen McGrody, "For Many Players, Lootboxes Are a Crisis That's Already Here," *Vice*, January 30, 2018. www.vice.com.

48. Quoted in McGrody, "For Many Players, Lootboxes Are a Crisis."

49. Quoted in Mike Ives, "Electroshock Therapy for Internet Addicts? China Vows to End It," *New York Times*, January 13, 2017. www.nytimes.com.

50. Quoted in Ives, "Electroshock Therapy for Internet Addicts?"

51. Quoted in Tom Gerken, "Video Game Loot Boxes Declared Illegal Under Belgium Gambling Laws," *BBC News*, April 26, 2018. www.bbc.co.uk.

52. Quoted in Gerken, "Video Game Loot Boxes Declared Illegal."

53. Quoted in Missy Keenan, "10 Tips: Help Kids Strike a Better Balance with Tech," *Des Moines Register*, April 25, 2015. www.demoinesregister.com.

54. Quoted in Chris Weller, "Bill Gates and Steve Jobs Raised Their Kids Tech-Free—And It Should've Been a Red Flag," *Independent*, October 24, 2017. www.independent.co.uk.

55. Peter Gray, "The Many Benefits, for Kids, of Playing Video Games," *Psychology Today*, January 7, 2012. www.psychologytoday.com.

56. Nanea Hoffman, "Why I Don't Limit Screen-Time for My Kids," *Washington Post*, May 18, 2015. www.washingtonpost.com.

57. Hoffman, "Why I Don't Limit Screen-Time for My Kids."

58. Rigby and Ryan, *Glued to Games*, p. 106.

59. Gray, "The Many Benefits, for Kids, of Playing Video Games."

60. Quoted in Dale Markowitz, "What It's Like to Finally Meet After Dating Online for Months," *Atlantic*, February 14, 2018. www.theatlantic.com.

61. Gray, "The Many Benefits, for Kids, of Playing Video Games."

62. "Let's Help Others Level Up—Our Cause," *Gamers Outreach*, April 12, 2018. www.gamersoutreach.com.

63. Quoted in Jessica Haynes, "Video Gamers Raise $722k for Young Hospital Patients at EMU Event," *MLive*, May 3, 2018. www.mlive.com.

64. Shu-Hsun Ho, Yu-Ling Lin, and Ruei-Hau Lee, "Exploring the Effective Help for Social Anxiety: MMORPGs Delivering Online Help," *International Journal of Marketing Studies*, 2015. www.ccsenet.org.

65. Quoted in University of Missouri-Columbia, "Children and Teens with Autism More Likely to Become Preoccupied with Video Games," *ScienceDaily*, April 17, 2013. www.sciencedaily.com.

66. Quoted in University of Missouri-Columbia, "Children and Teens with Autism."

67. Melanie Hempe, "Will Your Gamer Survive College?" *Psychology Today*, September 26, 2016. www.psychologytoday.com.

68. "From Fun Hobby to Divorce: How Gaming Addiction Impacted My Life," *Game Quitters*, n.d. www.gamequitters.com.

69. Greg Toppo, *The Game Believes in You*. New York: Palgrave MacMillan, 2015, p. 33.

70. LaShera McElhany, "The Hidden Value of Gaming in Education," *Thought Hub*, May 17, 2016. www.sagu.edu/thoughthub.

71. Quoted in "2017 Essential Facts about the Computer and Video Game Industry," *Entertainment Software Association*, 2017. www.theesa.com.

CHAPTER 4: THE FUTURE OF VIDEO GAME ADDICTION

72. Kardaras, Nicholas, "Screens in Schools are a $60 Billion Hoax," *Time*, August 31, 2016. www.time.com.

73. Kardaras, "Screens in Schools."

74. Quoted in Booth, "Internet Addiction Is Sweeping America."

75. Gilbert E. Franco, "Videogames and Therapy: A Narrative Review of Recent Publication and Application to Treatment," *Frontiers in Psychology*, July 14, 2016. www.frontiersin.org.

76. Quoted in Cosette Rae, "Virtual Reality: How Addictive Is It?" *reSTART*, n.d. www.netaddictionrecovery.com.

77. Quoted in Sarah Komadina, "Teens Sitting for Long Periods of Time Could Be Impacting Their Bone Health," *Global News*, April 5, 2017. www.globalnews.ca.

78. Quoted in Komadina, "Teens Sitting for Long Periods of Time."

79. Quoted in Justin Block, "Some Video Games Are Actually Good Exercise for Young Kids, Study Finds," *Huffington Post*, August 11, 2015. www.huffingtonpost.com.

80. "Our Guiding Principles," *reSTART*, n.d. www.netaddictionrecovery.com.

81. "How a Harmless Recreation Slowly Grew to Addiction," *reSTART*, June 24, 2015. www.netaddictionrecovery.com.

82. Kutner and Olson, *Grand Theft Childhood*, p. 161.

83. David Greenfield, "Tips for Mindful Technology Use," *Psychology Today*, October 21, 2017. www.psychologytoday.com.

FOR FURTHER RESEARCH

BOOKS

Laura Perdew, *Internet Addiction.* Minneapolis, MN: Abdo Publishing, 2015.

Ashley Strehle Hartman, *Youth and Video Games.* San Diego, CA: ReferencePoint Press, 2019.

Greg Toppo, *The Game Believes in You*. New York: Palgrave Macmillan Trade, 2015.

Stephanie Watson, *Video Game Designer*. San Diego, CA: ReferencePoint Press, 2018.

INTERNET SOURCES

"2017 Essential Facts About the Computer and Video Game Industry," *Entertainment Software Association*, 2017. www.theesa.com.

Barbara Booth, "Internet Addiction Is Sweeping America, Affecting Millions," *CNBC*, August 29, 2017. www.cnbc.com.

Peter Gray, "Sense and Nonsense About Video Game Addiction," *Psychology Today*, March 11, 2018. www.psychologytoday.com.

Nicholas Kardaras, "It's 'Digital Heroin': How Screens Turn Kids into Psychotic Junkies," *New York Post*, August 27, 2016. www.nypost.com.

Elena Malykhina, "Fact or Fiction: Video Games Are the Future of Education," *Scientific American*, September 12, 2014. www.scientificamerican.com.

Rebecca Robbins, "This Video Game May Help Kids with ADHD," *Scientific American*, December 5, 2017. www.scientificamerican.com.

RELATED ORGANIZATIONS AND WEBSITES

American Psychiatric Association

800 Maine Ave. SW, Suite 900
Washington D.C., 20024
apa@psych.org
www.psychiatry.org

The American Psychiatric Association (APA) is an organization of
psychiatrists that furthers research and education into mental illness and
substance use disorders.

Entertainment Software Association

601 Massachusetts Ave. NW, Suite 300
Washington, D.C. 20001
esa@theESA.com
www.theesa.com

The Entertainment Software Association (ESA) is a US association dedicated
to serving the business and public affairs needs of companies that publish
computer and video games.

reSTART

1001 290th Ave. SE
Fall City, WA 98024
connect@restartlife.com
www.restartlife.com

reSTART is a video game and internet addiction treatment center
in Washington.

World Health Organization

Avenue Appia 20
1211 Geneva 27, Switzerland
www.who.int

The World Health Organization (WHO) is the authority for international health
in the United Nations.

INDEX

INDEX CONTINUED

IMAGE CREDITS

ABOUT THE AUTHOR

P.J. Graham is a freelance education writer and blogger. She worked for more than twenty years as a writer and editor for an education company and several newspapers, writing educational activity books and user guides as well as feature articles and entertainment reviews. She lives in southeast Kansas with her family and several pets. In her spare time, she enjoys hiking, photography, gardening, hand drumming, role-playing games, and travel.